The [...] Joke Book

belongs to

_____

*Also available in Red Fox
(incorporating Beaver Books) by Janet Rogers:*

The Crazy, Crazy Joke Bag
The Joke-A-Day Fun Book

THE INCREDIBLY RUDE JOKE BOOK

JANET ROGERS

*Illustrated by
Vanessa Bergin*

RED FOX

A Red Fox Book
Published by Random Century Children's Books
20 Vauxhall Bridge Road, London SW1V 2SA

A division of the Random Century Group
London Melbourne Sydney Auckland
Johannesburg and agencies throughout the world

First published by Red Fox 1991

Text © Complete Editions 1991
Illustrations © Vanessa Bergin 1991

The right of Janet Rogers and Vanessa Bergin to be identified as the author and illustrator of this work has been asserted by them, in accordance with the Copyright, Designs and Patents Act, 1988.

This book is sold subject to the condition that it shall not, by way of trade or otherwise, be lent, resold, hired out, or otherwise circulated without the publisher's prior consent in any form of binding or cover other than that in which it is published and without a similar condition including this condition being imposed on the subsequent purchaser.

Set in Century Schoolbook
Typeset by JH Graphics Ltd, Reading

Printed and bound in Great Britain by
Cox & Wyman Ltd, Reading

ISBN 0 09 971090 0

CONTENTS

Introduction	7
Too naughty!	9
Don't be stupid!	22
Plain rude	37
Behaving badly	51
Backchat	65
Rude food	78
Rude rhymes	92
Plain yuck	98
Insulting behaviour	109

INTRODUCTION

Shhhhhhh! Can you keep a secret! You can? All right, but promise not to tell. The reason for all this secrecy is that this book contains a collection of the rudest, naughtiest, most disgusting jokes around — and your granny and your teacher probably won't like them!

You'll like them, I know, and so will your friends. But some of the jokes are a bit risky and if you tell them to the wrong people you might end up in trouble. Now I don't want you to get into hot water, so I've invented a safety system. If you look at the jokes you'll see that they're all marked with one star, two stars or three stars.

One star jokes ★ are jokes you can tell to anyone without having to worry about offending them. They're cheeky jokes — jokes that even your maiden aunt won't blush at.

And then there are two-star ★ ★ jokes, which are a bit more naughty and should be used with care. Don't tell them to your gran or the vicar unless you're absolutely sure they won't mind.

Last of all are the three-star ★ ★ ★ jokes, which are really rude! Your friends will love them, but don't go telling them to everyone or you'll cause a lot of red faces.

Now turn the pages and have a naughty giggle – but remember, be careful!

JANET ROGERS

TOO NAUGHTY!

Let's kick off with lots of lovely naughty jokes!

★ ★ ★ Why do bees fly around with their legs crossed?
'Cos they're looking for BP stations.

★ ★ ★ What floats on the sea shouting, 'Knickers'?
Crude oil.
And what floats on the sea shouting, 'Underwear!'?
Refined oil.

★ ★ What did the carpet say to the desk?
'I can see your drawers.'

★ ★ ★ How do you get an elephant in a matchbox?
First, take out the matches.
And how do you get Robbie Coltrane in a matchbox?
That's impossible...

★ ★ CANDY: I wish I had a penny for every boy who'd asked me out.
KATE: *Then you could afford to go to the loo!*

★ ★ CUSTOMER: Waiter, waiter! This hotpot isn't fit for a pig!
WAITER: *Very well, sir, I'll get you some that is.*

★ PATIENT: Doctor, doctor! I feel like a pair of scissors.
DOCTOR: *Just cut it out!*

★ ★ What animal do you look like when you get out of the bath?
A little bear.

★ ★ What happens when you cross an elephant with a carpet?
You get a thick pile all over the floor.

10

★ BILL: Did you hear about the man who went on holiday to France? He didn't like French food so he lived entirely on prunes.
BEN: *What happened to him?*
BILL: He spent the whole week in the Louvre.

★ CANDY: I wonder why Michael Jackson called his album 'Bad'?
KATE: *'Cos he couldn't spell 'awful.'*

★ What's the difference between Mrs Thatcher and an umbrella?
You can shut an umbrella up, but . . .

★ What did the idiot call his pet zebra?
Spot.

★★ BILL: Why are sardines so stupid?
BEN: *I don't know.*
BILL: 'Cos they climb into the can, close the lid – *and leave the key outside!*

★ What are furry and go eee-eee-eee when you eat them?
Mice Krispies.

★★ KATE: Do you like my new hairstyle?
CANDY: *It's brilliant – I can hardly see your face.*

★ Did you hear about the stupid man at the banana factory?
He kept throwing out the bent ones.

★★ What is black and white, then red all over?
A rabbit in a food processor.

★★ BILL: Keep that cat out of my mum's kitchen.
BEN: *Otherwise I suppose it'll be curry for lunch tomorrow . . .*

★ Why are the Queen's guardsmen rude?
'Cos they wear bearskins.

★ BILL: Have you heard that the cross-eyed teacher's got the sack?
BEN: *No, why?*
BILL: She couldn't control her pupils.

★ ★ What does a trade unionist do if his nose goes on strike?
Picket.

★ ★ BILL: Your girlfriend should have been born in the Dark Ages.
BEN: *Why's that?*
BILL: 'Cos she looks dreadful in daylight!

★ ★ ★ An Englishman was driving to Paris when he stopped to pick up a hitch-hiker by the side of the road. 'Do you want a lift?' he asked.
　'Oui, oui!' said the hitch-hiker.
　'Not in my car you don't!' said the Englishman and drove away.

★ ★ KATE: What's wrong with your teacher?
CANDY: *Nothing a funeral wouldn't cure.*

★ BILL: I wish you'd pay me just a little tiny bit of attention?
BEN: *I'm paying as little as I can.*

★ BILL: How do you spell idiot in one letter?
BEN: *I don't know.*
BILL: U.

★★ Which vegetables go to the loo?
Leeks and peas.

★★ CANDY: I went out with that new boy to see *The Vampire Zombie on Elm Street* last night.
KATE: *What was he like?*
CANDY: Disgusting – all white and pimply, with no front teeth and his hair standing on end.
KATE: *And what was your new boyfriend like?*
CANDY: That *was* him.

★ Which famous film star suffers from indigestion?
Burp Reynolds.

★ ★   What's white on the outside, green on the inside and wriggly when you eat it?
A caterpillar sandwich.

★ ★   BILL: What's your girlfriend's perfume called?
BEN: *High Heaven.*
BILL: Yuck! It stinks to it.

★   What do you call a fly with no wings?
A walk.

★ ★   Why did the seaweed blush?
Because it saw the Queen Elizabeth's *bottom.*

★ ★ ★   Is diarrhoea hereditary?
Yes, it runs in the genes.

★★ BILL: Imagine you're walking through the forest and suddenly this huge bear comes racing at you. What would you do — run a mile, jump a stile or eat a cowpat?
BEN: *I'd run a mile.*
BILL: What, with a bear behind?

★ KATE: What's the best way to Bath?
CANDY: *First take your clothes off.*

★ What happens when you cross a wimp and a sweet on a stick?
You get a wallypop.

★ PATIENT: Doctor, doctor! I've got terrible wind.
DOCTOR: *I've got just the thing for you. Here, take this kite . . .*

★★ BEN: I think God lives in our house.
BILL: *How do you know?*
BEN: 'Cos every morning my father bangs on the bathroom door and yells, 'God are you still in there?'

★ ★ What do you get if you sit under a cow?
A pat on the head.

★ ★ ★ BILL: What's the difference between a potty and a casserole dish?
BEN: *I don't know.*
BILL: I'm never coming to dinner at *your* house again!

★ ★ What's round and green and smells terrible?
Kermit's bottom.

★ CANDY: I'm not myself today.
KATE: *Yes, I noticed the improvement.*

★ ★ KATE: Have you tried those new paper knickers?
CANDY: *Yes, I did — and they're tearable.*

★ PATIENT: Doctor, doctor! I keep getting terrible headaches.
DOCTOR: *In that case we'll have to remove your brain.*
PATIENT: Will it help?
DOCTOR: *No, but it will keep your mind off the problem.*

★ CUSTOMER: Waiter, why is my food all mushed up and covered in mud?
WAITER: *Well, sir, you asked me to step on it.*

★ BEN: When did you discover your girlfriend had a glass eye?
BILL: *It just came out in conversation.*

★★ A little lad looked over the garden fence and saw his next-door neighbour spreading something on the garden. 'What are you doing?' he asked.

'I'm putting manure on my rhubarb,' said the neighbour.

'Yuck!' said the lad. 'We put custard on ours . . .'

★★   BILL: What would it take for you to kiss me?
     CANDY: *An anaesthetic.*

★   What's a sick joke?
     Something it's rude to bring up in conversation.

★   CANDY: My boyfriend's just said it with flowers.
     KATE: *Oh, how romantic!*
     CANDY: Not really – he just hit me on the head with a bunch of daffodils.

★★   What was the most difficult thing for a knight in armour to do?
     Scratch his bottom.

★   Knock, knock.
     Who's there?
     Dummy.
     Dummy who?
     Dummy a favour and get lost.

★★   What's the worst thing you can do to a girl wearing baggy underwear?
     Nick'er elastic.

★ ★ Why did the crab blush?
Because the seaweed.

★ BILL: Did you hear about the madman who keeps going round saying 'No' all the time?
BEN: *No.*
BILL: Aaagh – it's you!

★ What's the distance between a stupid person's ears?
Next to nothing.

★ CANDY: Would you kiss Ben for £5?
KATE: *No.*
CANDY: Would you kiss him for £10?
KATE: *No.*
CANDY: Would you kiss him for £20?
KATE: *No.*
CANDY: Then what would you kiss Bill for?
KATE: *Yuck! Nothing. . .*
CANDY: Oh, so you'd kiss Bill for nothing, would you?

★★ Knock, knock
Who's there?
Ivan.
Ivan who?
Ivan to go to the loo in a hurry!

★ KATE: I baked some cakes in the cookery class at school. Take your pick!
BEN: *I think a hammer and chisel would be better.*

DON'T BE STUPID!

Don't be stupid, stupid! Read these jokes and have a wicked laugh.

★ Did you hear about the stupid farmer who sowed razor blades with his potatoes? He wanted to grow chips.

★ CANDY: If two's company and three's a crowd, what's four and five?
KATE: *I don't know.*
CANDY: Nine, silly!

★ MRS NITWIT: You told me to drink this medicine after my bath, doctor, but I've got a problem.
DOCTOR: *What's that?*
MRS NITWIT: By the time I've drunk the bath I haven't got any room left for the medicine.

★ Did you hear about the stupid shoplifter? He was crushed under Woolworths.

★ KATE: What was the tallest mountain in the world before Mount Everest was discovered?
BEN: *I don't know.*
KATE: Mount Everest, stupid! It was the tallest whether it was discovered or not.

★ Did you hear about the stupid man who was asked to donate something to the new orphanage? He sent them three orphans.

★ KATE: If you have an umpire in tennis and a referee in football, what do you have in bowls?
BEN: *I don't know.*
KATE: Custard, stupid!

★ Candy, Ben and Bill were out one night and had a row.
'You're so stupid Candy!' said Bill.
'Come on,' said Ben, 'that's not nice. Say you're sorry.'
'All right,' said Bill. 'I'm sorry you're so stupid, Candy.'

★ ★ A nervous passenger was flying in a plane for the first time. 'How often do planes like this crash?' he asked the stewardess.
'Only once, stupid!' she replied.

★ BEN: Time seems to hang heavy on my hands these days.
BILL: *Then why don't you get a wristwatch instead of carrying around that grandfather clock all the time?*

★ CANDY: I wonder why the Queen doesn't wave with this hand?
BILL: *Because it's your hand silly!*

★ Have you heard about the fool who tried to cross the Atlantic on a plank? He had to give up when he couldn't find a plank long enough.

★ CANDY: People in London are stupid – and that's official.
KATE: *Why do you say that?*
CANDY: Because that's where the population is most dense.

★ BEN: Intelligence reigns supreme in my family
CANDY: *But it obviously didn't rain on the day you were born.*

★ Why did the painter wear all his clothes while he did the decorating?
Because on the tin it says, 'Apply three coats.'

★ KATE: Bill's just had his brain X-rayed.
CANDY: *What did they find?*
KATE: Nothing at all!

★ BEN: What's the difference between a monster and an orange?
CANDY: *I don't know.*
BEN: Have you ever tried peeling a monster?

★★ BILL: How many conkers grow on the average oak tree?
BEN: *A hundred?*
BILL: None, idiot! Conkers don't grow on oak trees.

★ Three identical men went into the car wash. How can you tell which one was stupid?
He was the one on a bicycle.

★ BEN: Is it possible to live without a brain?
CANDY: *How old are you?*

★ BILL: If it takes four men two days to dig a hole, how long will it take six men to dig half a hole?
BEN: *I don't know.*
BILL: You can't dig half a hole, stupid!

★ What do you call a thick vampire?
A stupid clot.

★ KATE: Ben's so stupid.
CANDY: *Why, what's he done now?*
KATE: He was ironing the curtains, and he fell out of the window.

You're so stupid . . .

. . . you think an autobiography is the life story of a car.

. . . you have to think twice before saying nothing.

. . . why don't you go home and brush up on your ignorance?

. . . that you could be an even bigger idiot if you had more brains.

. . . you think a fjord is a Scandinavian car.

. . . you're still looking for a sloping lake so that you can go water-skiiing.

★ KATE: Why don't you take a taxi home?
BILL: *Because my dad would make me take it back.*

★ KATE: Would you answer the door, please?
BILL: *I can't, I didn't hear the question.*

★★ What did the idiot do when he got a flea in his ear?
He shot it.

★★ Did you hear about the woman who was so stupid that when a visitor asked for a stiff drink she put cement in his tea?

★★ BEN: What's the difference between electricity and lightning?
CANDY: *I've no idea.*
BEN: When did you last get a lightning bill, stupid?

★ BEN: Why does everybody call me Bighead?
CANDY: *Don't worry – there's nothing in it!*

★ Why did Bill wear two shirts, two ties, two pairs of trousers and two jackets to the fancy-dress party?
Because he went as twins.

★ BEN: What are you going to do with that steel wool?
CANDY: *What do you think I'm doing — knitting a car?*

★★ KATE: Help! The collar of this blouse is so tight it's throttling me.
BILL: *Don't be stupid — you've put your head through the buttonhole!*

★★ Did you hear about the bimbo who always used toilet water? One day she banged her head on the toilet and had to go to hospital.

★ CANDY: Have you heard about the fool who bought a paper shop?
KATE: *No, what happened?*
CANDY: It blew away.

★ Did you hear about the idiot who went to the Italian restaurant and asked for an Italian?

★ Why did the stupid gardener pour beer on his lawn?
He wanted it to grow half cut.

★★ BILL: Why are you limping?
CANDY: *I went to the seaside yesterday and a crab pinched my toes.*
BILL: Which one?
CANDY: *How am I supposed to know? All crabs look the same to me.*

★★ BEN: I wouldn't say you're stupid . . .
KATE: *Thank you.*
BEN: But if you have an idea in your head, it's in solitary confinement.

★ CANDY: Which poet wrote 'To a Nightingale'?
KATE: *I don't know — but whoever it was, I bet he didn't get a reply.*

★★ CANDY: You're so stupid, you should join the FBI.
BEN: *The Federal Bureau of Investigation?*
CANDY: No, the Feather-Brained Idiots!

★★ MR NITWIT: Our son was so stupid he had a brain transplant.
BEN: *And did it work?*
MR NITWIT: No, the brain rejected him.

★ What happened to the idiot who wanted to listen to the match?
He burned his ear.

★★ BILL: I could be a famous scientist if only I had the mind to
KATE: *Yes, the only thing you need is a mind, really.*

★ What's at the top of an idiot's ladder?
A sign saying 'stop'.

★ KATE: How do you get two whales in a Mini?
BEN: *You can't.*
KATE: Yes you can – you just go over the Severn Bridge.

★ A stupid dragon went to see the doctor with a terrible stomach ache. 'Hmm,' said the doctor, 'it could be salmonella. What have you had to eat lately?'

'I had a knight in armour the other day,' said the dragon.

'And did you check he was fresh before you ate him?'

'You mean I was supposed to take him out of his armour first?'

★ CANDY: My brother's so stupid!
   BEN: *What did he do?*
   CANDY: He wanted to go hitch-hiking, so he left the house early before there was too much traffic around.

★ What's white and flies upwards?
   A stupid snowflake.

★ BEN: Did you hear about the stupid dog?
   KATE: *No, tell me.*
   BEN: It lay down to chew a bone and when it got up it only had three legs.

★ What did the idiot say when the driver asked him to check whether his car indicators were working?
   'Yes, no, yes, no, yes, no, yes, no . . .'

★ Have you heard about the stupid man who wanted to know how long it takes to fly to Miami? He phoned the travel agent and asked, 'How long does it take to fly to Miami?'
   'Just a minute,' said the travel agent.
   'Thanks,' said the idiot and put the phone down.

★ BEN: Do you have holes in your trousers?
BILL: *No, of course not.*
BEN: Then how do you get your legs in them?

★ Did you hear about the stupid farmer who ploughed his field with a steam-roller? He wanted to grow mashed potatoes.

★★ KATE: Why did Robin Hood rob the rich?
BILL: *He'd have to be pretty stupid to rob the poor, wouldn't he?*

★ KATE: Which of these is grammatically correct? 'The white of an egg *is* yellow' or 'The white of an egg *are* yellow'?
CANDY: *The white of an egg is yellow.*
KATE: Don't be stupid – the white of an egg is white!

★ BILL: I just failed my exams to become an undertaker.
CANDY: *Too stiff, eh?*

★ BEN: How did you burn your ear?
BILL: *I was doing the ironing when the phone rang.*

★★ How do you make an idiot laugh on Sunday?
Tell him a joke on Friday night.

★ MRS NITWIT: Did you put the cat out?
MR NITWIT: *It wasn't on fire again, was it?*

★★ KATE: What do you think is the height of stupidity?
BEN: *How tall are you?*

34

★ A girl at school opened her packed lunch and took out the top sandwich. 'Yuck! It's tuna,' she said. 'I hate tuna,' and threw it in the bin. She picked up the next sandwich. 'Eeugh! Sardine and marmalade, I can't eat that!' And she chucked that one in the bin too. She picked up the third sandwich and sniffed it. 'Pooh! It's smelly blue cheese − I couldn't possibly swallow that!'

'Hasn't your mum packed you anything that you like?' asked the girl sitting next to her.

'Oh, my mother doesn't make my sandwiches,' came the reply. 'I make them myself.'

★★ Ben's father is so stupid he couldn't tell porridge from putty − which is why all the windows fell out.

★ BILL: Why is your shirt so wet?
BEN: *The label on it says 'Wash and wear', so I am.*

★ CANDY: Why was the Frenchman buried at the top of the mountain?
KATE: *I've no idea.*
CANDY: Because he was dead, stupid!

★ ★ Two mountaineers went climbing Mount Everest. Halfway up one of them fell from a ledge and broke both his wrists. 'What am I going to do?' he moaned to his friend.

'I'll pull you to safety,' said the friend. 'All you have to do is hold on to this rope with your teeth.' So the injured man gripped the rope with his teeth and slowly, inch by inch, his friend began to haul him back up. It took ages, but at last the injured mountaineer approached the rock on which his partner was sitting safely, pulling at the rope. 'Are you all right?' asked the rescuer as his friend came into view.

'Ye . . . aaaaaaaaaaagh!'

PLAIN RUDE

Be careful who you tell these jokes to. The vicar or your granny probably won't like them, but your friends will think they're terrific!

★ ★ What's the difference between a snooper and someone who's just got out of the bath?
One is rude and nosey and the other's nude and rosy.

★ BILL: I wouldn't say my mum's mean ...
BEN: *But she keeps a fork in the sugar bowl!*

★ ★ Knock, knock.
Who's there?
Ivy.
Ivy who?
Ivy seen your underwear.

★ CANDY: I don't believe all this rubbish about hairdos and make-up. I believe that everybody's naturally beautiful.
BILL: *In the dark, maybe . . .*

★ How do you double the price of a Lada?
Install a radio.

★ ★ KATE: This year I'm going to change everything about me — my hairstyle, my job, my wardrobe . . .
CANDY: *And don't forget your knickers.*

★ ★ CANDY: Have you ever seen that statue called 'The Thinker'?
BILL: *Yes.*
CANDY: I wonder what he's thinking about?
BILL: *I expect he's wondering how he's going to get home without any clothes on.*

★ ★ What's the rudest letter of the alphabet?
P.

★ ★ PATIENT: Doctor, doctor! I've only got 59 seconds to live!
DOCTOR: *Sit down and shut up for a minute, will you?*

★ ★ One day near Christmas a boy came racing into the house and straight into the lounge where his dad was watching television. 'Dad, Dad!' he cried, 'I've got my eye on this brilliant bike for Christmas!'

'Well, you can keep your eye on it,' said his father, 'but you're not going to get your bottom on it!'

★ BEN: What has a head and no brain, but still drives?
KATE: *Bill?*
BEN: Well, yes . . . but I was actually thinking of a golf club.

★ What kind of tree can't you climb?
A lavatory.

★ CANDY: I believe anything is possible.
BILL: *That's only because you don't know what you're talking about.*

★★ How should you describe two policeman on the beat?
A pair of nickers.

★ What do you call an open-top Lada?
A skip.

★ PATIENT: Doctor, doctor! I'm at death's door!
DOCTOR: *Then I'll pull you through.*

★★ Ben gave his little sister a bottle of perfume for her birthday and she kept dabbing it on her wrists and behind her ears. As a special treat her parents said she could stay up late for a dinner party with their friends. The guests arrived and soon everyone went to sit down in the dining-room. Ben's little sister had been placed between two of their parents' friends. As they sat down at the table she tugged their sleeves and said, 'If you hear a little noise and smell a little smell, it's only me.'

★ DOCTOR: I'm awfully sorry but I can't see what's wrong with you. It must be something to do with the drink.
BEN: *All right, I'll come back when you're sober.*

★★★ How can you tell the sex of a hormone?
You have to take its genes off.

★ ★ Knock, knock.
Who's there?
Ahab.
Ahab who?
Ahab to go to the loo right now!

★ Why do Wales always win at rugby?
'Cos they're socks are so smelly no one will tackle them.

★ BILL: MFI have merged with Tesco.
BEN: *How do you know that?*
BILL: I just bought a chicken and when I got it home its legs fell off.

★ Why do Ladas have heated rear windows?
To warm the hands of the people who have to push them.

★   KATE: What do you want for your birthday?
    BILL: *I'd like a surprise.*
    KATE: Okay – BOO.

★   PATIENT: Doctor, doctor! I get a terrible pain if I lift my arm in the air!
    DOCTOR: *Then don't put your arm in the air, stupid!*

★   Mr Nitwit was on the phone to his wife. 'I missed you last week, darling,' he said. 'When are you coming home.'
    'So that you can greet me with a big kiss?' asked Mrs Nitwit.
    'No, so that I can take another shot at you.'

★★ Which French town has two lavatories in each house?
    Toulouse.

★★★ What, put in the middle of pies, makes it difficult to sit down?
    L – because it turns pies into piles.

★   What do you call a bear who doesn't use a deodorant?
    Winnie the Pooh.

★ ★ ★   Mum, now I'm sixteen can I wear make-up and mini-skirts and go out with boys?
No, Nigel, you can't.

★ ★ ★   BILL: Doctor, I keep losing my temper.
DOCTOR: *Pardon?*
BILL: I said I keep losing my temper, you bald-headed, dozy old twit!

★   What is a Skoda owner's instruction manual called?
A bus timetable.

★   Which nursery-rhyme character lives with her granny and swears a lot?
Little Rude Riding-Hood.

★ ★   What should you call two red roses?
A pair of bloomers.

★ ★   Knock, knock.
Who's there?
Nicholas.
Nicholas who?
Nicholas girls should never climb trees.

★   What do you get if you pull your knickers up to your chin?
A chest of drawers.

★ ★ ★   MR NITWIT: This amazing chicken lays square eggs the size of bricks.
CANDY: *That's incredible.*
MR NITWIT: And it speaks, too.
CANDY: *What does it say?*
MR NITWIT: Aaaaagh, my bum!

★ ★ ★   Why did the boy scratch his bottom?
Because he was the only one who knew where the itch was.

★ ★ ★   A policeman was walking through the park on patrol one day when he came across a young vandal holding a puppy by the scruff of its neck and shaking it. 'Stop that immediately!' said the policeman. 'Whatever you do to that poor puppy, I'll do the same to you.'

'In that case,' said the vandal . . . and gave the puppy a big smacking kiss.

★ ★   Knock, knock.
Who's there?
Arfur.
Arfur who?
Arfur got to put my trousers on this morning!

★   How do you make a loo roll?
Push it down a mountain.

★   CANDY: Sorry, my mind's wandering.
    KATE: *Don't worry, it's too weak to get very far.*

★   PATIENT: Doctor, doctor! I feel like a soft drink.
    DOCTOR: *How many times have I told you not to play squash?*

★ ★ ★   BILL: I phoned Buckingham Palace the other day.
    CANDY: *Did you get through to the Queen?*
    BILL: No, they said she was on the throne and couldn't be disturbed.

★   What do you call a Skoda with twin exhausts?
    A wheelbarrow.

★ ★   Two pigeons were flying around London when beneath them they saw an amazing car for sale. 'Wow, look at that Ferrari!' said one.
    'I know,' said the other. 'Why don't we go and put a deposit on it?'

★ ★ ★   What did Prince Charles say when Prince William was rude to the footman?
    'If you don't shut up I'll crown you!'

★ ★ ★ It was election time and a political canvasser was knocking on doors to find out which way people intended to vote. When he knocked on one door it was opened by a little girl. 'Can Mummy come to the door?' he asked her. The little girl shook her head. 'In that case, do you know whether your mummy's in the Green Party or the Labour Party or the Conservative Party?' asked the man.

'She's not in any of them,' said the girl. 'She's in the loo.'

★ ★ PATIENT: Doctor, doctor! I've got a temperature – I'm boiling!
DOCTOR: *Stop fussing and simmer down.*

★ KATE: My little brother's got such an infectious smile.
BILL: *Well, don't let him smile anywhere near me!*

★ ★ What do you call a stupid person with two panes of glass on his head?
Paddy O'Doors.

★ ★ Knock, knock.
Who's there?
Andrew.
Andrew who?
Andrew a naughty picture of teacher on the blackboard.

★ ★ MRS NITWIT: How old would you say I am?
BILL: *About 40.*
MRS NITWIT: And how do you work that out?
BILL: *Well, my sister's 20, and you're twice as stupid as she is . . .*

★ ★ A boy was standing at a bus stop eating a burger and chips. Next to him in the queue was a woman with a Yorkshire terrier on a lead. The Yorkshire terrier kept yapping and jumping up and down, trying to get a piece of burger. Eventually the boy said to the woman, 'Would you mind if I chucked him a bit?'

'Oh, no,' said the woman. 'He'd like that!'

So the boy picked up the dog and chucked it over the fence.

★ ★ CANDY: Why does your grandpa sleep under the bed?
BEN: *He thinks he's a little potty.*

★ ★ ★ What do boys with spots have in common with non-slip rugs?
They both have pimples on their bottoms.

★ BILL: Do you like my cake?
KATE: *Did you buy it yourself?*

★ ★ What's the definition of a harp?
A piano with no clothes on.

★ ★ CUSTOMER: Waiter, waiter! This fish tastes funny.
WAITER: *So why aren't you laughing?*

★ KATE: Your pet mouse stinks
BILL: *What it needs is a mousewash.*

★ ★ ★ Knock, knock.
Who's there?
Luke.
Luke who?
Luke through the keyhole and you'll see me in the bath!

★ ★ What do you call an American who spends hours on the loo?
John.

★ BILL: Did you hear about the cannibal who went to the circus?
KATE: *I don't approve of cannibal jokes.*
BILL: Why not?
KATE: *Because they're in bad taste.*

★ PATIENT: Doctor, Doctor! I keep thinking I'm a fridge.
DOCTOR: *Well, shut your door – your light's shining in my eyes.*

★ ★ ★ Knock, Knock.
Who's there?
Sawyer.
Sawyer who?
Sawyer with no clothes on yesterday!

★ ★ KATE: How old is your mum?
BILL: *I'm not sure, but she had so many candles on her birthday cake last year that the fire brigade were on emergency standby.*

★ A man was going round from door to door selling things. At one house he knocked and a woman answered. 'Would you like to buy a dustpan and brush?' asked the salesman.

'No,' said the woman.

'Some dusters and polish?'

'No,' said the woman.

'A scrubbing brush?'

'No,' said the woman.

'A carpet cleaner?'

'No,' said the woman.

'I didn't think so,' said the salesman with a sigh. 'The woman next door told me you never clean your house.'

BEHAVING BADLY

All these jokes are about behaving badly or being rude — and of course you're never badly-behaved or cheeky, are you? I've found that if you're wickedly funny you can get away with almost anything. You don't believe it? Check these jokes out.

★ BILL: Girls keep whispering they love me.
BEN: *That's because none of them dare to say it out loud.*

★ Should you eat roast beef on an empty stomach?
No, you should eat it off a plate.

★★ BILL: I'd like a return ticket, please.
TICKET CLERK: *Where to?*
BILL: Back here, stupid!

★ What did the robot say to the petrol pump?
Don't you know it's rude to stick your finger in your ear when I'm talking to you?'

★★ CANDY: Did you miss me while I was away?
BILL: *Oh, have you been away?*

★ CUSTOMER: Waiter, waiter! I'd like a table.
WAITER: *And how do you want it – boiled, baked or fried?*

★★ A little boy had been taken by his mum to see Santa Claus at a local department store. 'Ho, ho, ho!' said Santa. 'And what would you like for Christmas, young man?'

'I wrote and told you last week, you stupid idiot, and you've forgotten already!' the boy replied.

★★ MRS NITWIT: I hear you rescued my son Nigel when he fell in the river;
BILL *(modestly): Yes, I did – but it was nothing.*
MRS NITWIT: There's only one thing I have to say to you – where's his school cap?

★ Does Frankenstein's monster have good table manners?
No, he bolts his food down.

★ KATE: Did you go to school, stupid?
BEN: *Yes, and I came back stupid as well.*

★ A young boy saw his big sister having a kiss and a cuddle with her boyfriend, so the next day he went looking for the boyfriend. 'I saw you kissing my sister last night,' he said.

'Look,' said the boyfriend, 'if I give you £1 will you promise not to tell your mum and dad?'

'It'll cost you £5,' said the boy.

'But that's incredibly expensive,' said the boyfriend.

'It's what all the other lads give me.'

★★ CANDY: My mum's so well-mannered. She never says anything unkind about anyone.
BILL: *Only because she never stops talking about herself.*

★ Did you hear about the bad-mannered taxi driver? He drove all his customers away.

★ BEN: I've made the chicken soup.
KATE: *Thank goodness — I thought we were going to have to eat it!*

★ 'This is the most amazing parrot you've ever seen,' said the pet-shop owner. 'If you pull its right leg it will sing the National Anthem, and if you pull its left leg it will sing 'Happy Birthday'.
'That's incredible!' said the man who'd come in to take a look at the parrot. He lifted the bird's right leg and sure enough it began

to sing 'God save our gracious Queen . . .' 'I'll buy it,' said the man.

When he got home he showed the parrot to his wife and explained what it had been trained to do. 'I don't believe it,' said the wife. So she pulled its right leg. 'God save our gracious Queen . . .' warbled the parrot. Then she pulled its left leg. 'Happy Birthday to you . . .' it sang.

'That's amazing,' said the wife. 'I wonder what happens if you pull both its legs at the same time?'

'I bloomin' well fall over on my back, stupid!' shrieked the parrot.

★ CANDY: Do you think I'm pretty?
BEN: *In a way you are.*
CANDY: What way?
BEN: *As far away as possible.*

★ A boy sat on the bus chewing gum rudely with his mouth wide open. After a while an old lady leaned across to him and said very loudly, 'It's no use talking to me like that — I'm deaf.'

★★ MOTHER BEAR: Who's been eating my porridge?
FATHER BEAR: *Who's been eating my porridge?*
BABY BEAR: Burp!

★ MUM: You're not to keep saying that Mr Shufflebottom's bald. It's very rude.
BEN: *Then what should I say?*
MUM: That he has a very wide parting.

★★ CUSTOMER: Waiter, waiter! There's a dead cockroach in my soup!
WAITER: *Well, what do you expect for these prices?*

★ The Queen had just been introduced to a new servant. 'I shall see you tomorrow,' said Her Majesty. 'Breakfast is at 8 am prompt.'

'Very well, ma'am,' said the new servant. 'And if I oversleep, you can start without me.'

★★ A boy was travelling on a bus one day when a very large lady got on. There were no more seats and she looked at him accusingly and said, 'If you had any manners, young man, you'd get up and let me sit down.'

'And if *you* had any manners,' said the boy, '*you'd* stay standing and allow three others to sit down.'

★ ★ ★ Knock, knock.
Who's there?
Doughnut.
Doughnut who?
Doughnut forget to change your knickers.

★ MRS NITWIT: Go outside and play football with your brother.
NIGEL NITWIT: *When am I going to get a real football to play with?*

★ Mr and Mrs Nitwit went on holiday to Blackpool. One day they went on a trip to the Lake District in their car and on their way home they had a breakdown. It was very late when they got back to their guest house and the door was locked. Mr Nitwit rang the bell and an upstairs window flew open and the landlady looked out.

'What do you want?' she asked crossly.

'We're the Nitwits – we're staying here,' said Mr Nitwit.

'Okay, you stay there!' said the landlady – and slammed the window.

★ KATE: You'll have to accept my opinion for what it's worth.
CANDY: *In that case you owe me 50p.*

★ ★ The dustmen were just about to finish collecting all the garbage in a street when a girl came running out of one of the houses carrying a bag full of rubbish. 'Is it too late for rubbish?' she called.

'No!' yelled one of the dustmen. 'Just get in!'

★ ★ Kate went to the doctor because she had a sore throat. 'Would you go to the window and stick your tongue out,' said the doctor.

'Why, Doctor?' asked Kate.

'Because I hate the woman who lives in the house opposite.'

★ MRS MONSTER: Your table manners are terrible! Don't use your fingers to eat.
LITTLE MONSTER: *What* should *I use?*
MRS MONSTER: A spade.

★ Why are horses so bad-mannered?
They go to bed with their shoes on.

★ At a restaurant in the jungle one lunchtime a spotted green loud-mouthed frog was hopping from table to table making a nuisance of himself. 'What do you like to eat for lunch, Baboon?' he asked, jumping up and down on the baboon's plate.

'I like bananas and mangoes,' said the baboon. The frog hopped off, SPLAT! into the giraffe's pudding.

'Tell me, Giraffe!' he yelled, 'what's your favourite kind of food?'

'I like leaves and hay,' said the giraffe crossly.

The frog jumped to the floor and then up on to the tiger's table. 'And what do you like to eat, Tiger?' he asked.

'Well, first of all I'm *Mr* Tiger to you,' said the tiger. 'And to answer your question, I like to eat little spotted green loud-mouthed frogs.'

'Oh,' whispered the little green loud-mouthed frog, 'you don't see many of those around, do you?'

★ ★   DOCTOR: May I take your pulse?
CANDY: *Why, haven't you got one of your own?*

★   Who are the rudest people in Fairyland?
The goblins – they have terrible table manners.

★   MUM: Why have you been sent home from school early?
KATE: *The boy sitting next to me in Maths was smoking.*
MUM: But why were *you* sent home if *he* was smoking?
KATE: *I was the one who set him alight.*

★   Mr Nitwit was stopped in the street by a tramp. 'Can you help me, Guvnor,' he asked. 'I haven't had a bite all day.'
So Mr Nitwit bit him.

★ ★   GRANDAD: Behave yourself! Don't you know where bad boys and girls go?
BILL: *Yes, behind the bike shed.*

★ ★   Ben went to the cinema. Halfway through the film he decided he wanted some popcorn to eat, so he squeezed along the row to get out. A few minutes later he came down the aisle in the dark and stopped by a man at the end of a row.

'Excuse me,' he said, 'did I just tread on your foot as I went past?'

'Yes,' said the man.

'Good,' said Ben. 'I've got the right row.'

★★ BEN: Let's play a game of skill and wit.
KATE: *Oh no, let's play something you can join in with.*

★★ CUSTOMER: Waiter, Waiter! This egg is bad!
WAITER: *Don't moan at me — I only laid the table.*

★ CANDY: What does your mother call your father?
BEN: *Nothing — she likes him.*

★★ 'Bill, your manners are terrible!' said Mum. 'Instead of reaching right across the table for the tomato sauce, why don't you use your tongue?'

'But my tongue's not long enough to reach it!'

★★ BEN: I wouldn't say Candy's got a big mouth, but . . .
BILL: *But what?*
BEN: She's the only person I know who can eat a banana sideways.

★ Why are sausages bad-mannered?
'Cos they spit at the grill.

★ The three bears came down to breakfast one lovely spring morning. 'Who's been eating my porridge?' asked Father Bear, looking down at his empty dish. 'And who's been eating *my* porridge?' squeaked Baby Bear, looking down at his empty dish.

'Stop complaining, you two!' said Mother Bear. 'I haven't made it yet.'

★ KATE: My big brother speaks seven different languages.
BEN: *And he can't say 'please' and 'thank you' in any of them.*

★★ Mum came home one afternoon and found her kids and their friends sitting around the kitchen table. In the middle was a big bag of crisps. 'What are you doing?' she asked.

'We're having a competition,' said her son. 'The person who tells the biggest lie gets the crisps.'

'That's dreadful,' said Mum. 'I'm shocked! When I was your age I didn't know what a lie was, let alone tell them!

The kids sighed. 'All right, Mum, you get the crisps.'

★★ BILL: I wish you'd tell your little sister not to keep doing rude imitations of me.
CANDY: *I have — I told her not to behave like a stupid idiot.*

★ MUM: Go and wash your face. I can see what you had for lunch.
BEN: *What was it?*
MUM: Stew — I can see the gravy stains.
BEN: Wrong — I had stew the day before yesterday.

★ What did the cat do after it had eaten four mice?
It burped.

★ BILL: I'm not rich like Martin, I don't have a castle like Jason or a Porsche like Gavin, but I love you and I want you to marry me.
KATE: *And I love you — but what did you say about Jason?*

★ KATE: This stew's half cold.
CANDY: *Then eat the half that's hot.*

★★ Two little girls were talking in the school playground. 'I know a way of finding out how old our teacher is,' said one of them.

'How?' asked the other.

'All we have to do is get a pair of her knickers.'

'And how will that help?'

'Well, my knickers have a label saying 6–8 years old.'

BACKCHAT

There is nothing better than a quick line of cheeky backchat — but be careful who you try it out on. Your friends won't mind if you're cheeky to them but your parents and your teacher won't be so keen!

★ BILL: Do you believe in free speech?
CANDY: *Of course I do.*
BILL: Then you won't mind if I use your phone.

★★ CANDY: I always say a friend in need...
BILL: ... *is a pest.*

★★ BEN: What do you call a woman who owns two lavatories?
KATE: *Lulu.*

★ KATE: Ben's just bought a pair of trousers from MFI.
CANDY: *How do you know they're from MFI.*
KATE: He had to wait six weeks for them to be delivered and the next day they fell apart.

★ PROUD MUM: His teachers say Bill will soon get ahead.
BEN: *Good, because he looks odd without anything on top of his neck.*

★ CANDY: Do you like this hat? It's more than fifty years old!
KATE: *And did you make it yourself?*

★★ BILL: I'd go to the ends of the earth for you.
KATE: *Off you go then!*

★ KATE: My mum's sponge cakes are wonderfully light.
BEN: *It must have something to do with all the petrol she puts in them.*

★ PATIENT: Doctor, doctor! I keep thinking I'm a ball of string.
DOCTOR: *Then get knotted.*

★ CANDY: Mrs Nitwit is a brilliant business woman.
BEN: *Does she run her own company?*
CANDY: No, but her nose is always in other people's business.

★ MR NITWIT: Who was that at the door?
MRS NITWIT: *A boy with a drum.*
BEN: Then tell him to beat it.

★ BEN: I like your Christmas tie.
BILL: *Why do you call it my Christmas tie?*
BEN: 'Cos it's got roast turkey and cranberry sauce down it.

★ CANDY: I like the simple things in life.
KATE: *Like Bill . . .*

★ BEN: Why have you got a sticking plaster on the top of your head?
KATE: *I bit myself.*
BEN: How on earth did you bite yourself on the top of your head?
KATE: *I climbed a ladder.*

★ ★ BILL: You'd made a perfect . . .
CANDY: *A perfect what? Girlfriend?*
BILL: No, a perfect stranger.

★★ BEN: Your new boyfriend's a fishmonger, isn't he?
KATE: *How did you know that?*
BEN: There's a certain air about him . . .

★★ CANDY: When my dad speaks, people stand open-mouthed listening to his conversation.
BILL: *Yes, it's impossible to stop yawning.*

★ TEACHER: You missed school yesterday, Candy.
CANDY: *No I didn't – not for a single minute!*

★ KATE: You can't sleep in that bed – it's full of fleas!
BEN: *I don't care! They'll just have to make room for me.*

★ MRS NITWIT: I hate flying in planes.
MR NITWIT: *Well, I'd hate flying without one.*

★ CANDY: Why were you sacked from your Saturday job?
BILL: *Sickness.*
CANDY: You mean they sacked you because you were ill?
BILL: *No — because the sight of me made my boss sick.*

★★ CUSTOMER: Waiter, waiter! That curry was so hot it's given me heartburn!
WAITER: *Well, what did you expect — sunburn?*

★ BEN: I like your new abstract painting.
BILL: *It's not a painting — it's a mirror.*

★★ KATE: Ben is good at everything he does.
CANDY: *And from what I've seen, he usually does nothing.*

★ BILL: What do you think of the Venus de Milo?
KATE: *I suppose she's perfectly 'armless.*

★ BEN: My neighbours just had a visit from the man from Littlewoods.
CANDY: *Wow! Have they won the football pools?*
BEN: No, they were caught shoplifting.

★★ Dreadful Auntie Aggie was staying with her relatives, much to the disgust of her niece. Finally, after a week, Aunt Aggie announced, 'I think I'll go home tomorrow. Will you be sorry?'

'Yes,' said her niece, looking sad. 'I thought you might go today.'

★★ MRS NITWIT: My husband asked for an electrical gadget for Christmas.
MRS SHUFFLEBOTTOM: *How about an electric chair?*

★★ CANDY: You have to take Bill at face value.
BEN: *And with a face like his, that's not worth much.*

★ PATIENT: Well, doctor, how do I stand?
DOCTOR: *It's a mystery to me.*

★   CANDY: Do you think there's intelligent life on earth?
BILL: *Yes, but I'm only visiting.*

★   MR NITWIT: Who was at the door?
MRS NITWIT: *A man with one leg.*
MR NITWIT: Then tell him to hop it!'

★ ★   HOTEL PORTER: Can I carry your bag for you, sir?
GUEST: *No thanks. My wife can walk.*

★ ★   A cheeky boy raced into a baker's shop just before closing time one day 'Have you got any buns left?' he asked.
'Yes,' said the baker.
'Serves you right for baking too many!'

★ ★   KATE: My sister's boyfriend is an expert on Ancient Greece.
BEN: *How do you know?*
KATE: He never washes his hair.

★   BILL: I work on Saturday afternoon for Mr Shufflebottom, and I really admire him.
KATE: *And if you didn't you'd be fired.*

★ CANDY: Is it true you're marrying Susie just because her grandpa died and left her a million pounds?
BEN: *No, I would be marrying her whoever had left her a million!*

★ Have you heard about the man who's so clumsy that when he falls over he misses the floor?

★★ GRANDMA: What did you say when Mrs Jones gave you an ice-cream?
NAUGHTY KID: *'Take the wrapper off!'*

★ KATE: Can you help me out?
BEN: *Which way did you come in?*

★ CANDY: You've got to hand it to my dad – he's got real polish.
BILL: *But only on his shoes.*

★★ BEN: Help! I'm stuck on this homework question. What does 'opaque' mean!
CANDY: *It describes something through which light can't pass, like your skull.*

★ KATE: Bill's a real worm!
CANDY: *Yes, and he thinks we worship the ground he slithers across.*

★★ CANDY: Do you think clumsiness is catching?
KATE: *No, clumsiness is dropping, stupid!*

★ BILL: Hey, stop the bus! someone's just fallen off!
BUS CONDUCTOR: *Don't worry – he'd already paid his fare.*

★★ KATE: Ben's a real gentleman. He never hits a man when he's down.
CANDY: *Just in case he gets up again!*

★ BILL: My sister's gone to the West Indies.
BEN: *Jamaica?*
BILL: No, she went voluntarily.

★ KATE: My mum says I have an infectious smile.
BEN: *Then keep away from me!*

★ CANDY: Ben's cut out to be a great actor.
KATE: *Maybe, but what a pity no one bothered to put the bits together.*

★★ PATIENT: Doctor, doctor! I've lost my appetite. Can you give me something to sharpen it?
DOCTOR: *How about a razor blade?*

★ MR NITWIT: Who was that at the door?
MRS NITWIT: *A woman with a pram.*
MR NITWIT: Just tell her to push off!

★★ BILL: This photo you took doesn't do me justice.
BEN: *It's not justice you need, it's mercy.*

★ BEN: Kate says I'm the biggest liar in the world.
CANDY: *I don't believe you.*

★★ CUSTOMER: Waiter, waiter! There's a film on this stew!
WAITER: *Well, shut up and watch it.*

★ BILL: When you first speak to my dad he probably seems a bit of a bore.
CANDY: *And when you get to know him properly he's a real bore.*

★ BILL: I have this amazing effect on women. Whenever I pass a girl she sighs.
KATE: *With relief.*

★ ★ BEN: Say those three little words that would make me a happy man.
KATE: *All right – push off home!*

★ CANDY: Bill's so lazy.
KATE: *Ben's worse. He sticks his nose outside the window so the wind can blow it for him.*

★ ★ BEN: I'm going to join Friends of the Earth and fight air and water pollution.
BILL: *You could start by not breathing or taking baths.*

★ DENTIST: Have your teeth ever been checked?
BEN: *No, they've always been white.*

★ BILL: I hate graffiti.
BEN: *I hate all foreign food!*

★ CANDY: Ben's such a deep person.
  KATE: *Yes, he's deeply ignorant.*

★★ BILL: My mum's one in a million.
   BEN: *Thank goodness for that!*

★ CANDY: All right, all right, I admit I can be temperamental!
  BEN: *You said it – half bad-tempered and half mental.*

★★ KATE: Ben had his photo taken yesterday but the photographer hasn't developed it yet.
   BILL: *Why not?*
   KATE: He's too frightened to be alone in the darkroom with it!

★ CANDY: My dad's teeth are like the ten commandments.
  BEN: *Why's that?*
  CANDY: They're all broken.

★★ CANDY: My little brother's a thief, a liar and a cheat!
   BEN: *He's improving!*

★ KATE: I've met a new boy who's really nice — but he's got cross-eyes.
CANDY: *Never mind! At least he can watch a tennis match without moving his head.*

★★ BILL: I just have to spend a few minutes with Kate and I'm jumping for joy.
BEN: *I just have to spend a few minutes with her and I feel like jumping out of the window.*

★ KATE: Why do you call Candy 'Owl'?
BILL: *Because she doesn't give a hoot about me.*

★★ BILL: Shall I do an impression of Candy singing?
BEN: *Go on then.*
BILL: Hold on a second while I pinch my fingers in the door.

★ KATE: My mum says my dad's a miracle worker.
BILL: *He performs miracles, does he?*
KATE: No — but it's a miracle if he does any work.

★★ Bill and Ben were throwing stones at the Nitwits' greenhouse. 'You young terrors!' cried Mr Nitwit. 'Wait till I get my hands on you — I'll teach you to throw stones.'
'Yes, please,' said Ben. 'We've been trying all afternoon and we haven't managed to hit it yet.'

RUDE FOOD

Don't read these jokes if you've just had your dinner (or if you're going to have your dinner in a few minutes), because some of them are distinctly disgusting.

★ ★ ★ What's the difference between a Brussels sprout and a bogey?
Kids won't eat Brussels sprouts.

★ Why is spaghetti bolognese so rude?
It's got a lot of sauce.

★ ★ CUSTOMER: Waiter, waiter! There's a fly in my soup.
WAITER: *Well, you'll have to get it out yourself – I can't swim.*

★★ KATE: I've found a new café where you can eat dirt cheap.
CANDY: *Well, you* may *want to eat dirt . . .*

★★ CUSTOMER: Waiter, waiter! What's this?
WAITER: *It's bean soup.*
CUSTOMER: I don't care what it's been — what is it now.

★ Why did the milk blush?
Because it saw the salad dressing.

★★ BEN: I wouldn't say Kate is stupid, but . . .
BILL: *But what?*
BEN: When she wanted to make Scotch eggs she went down to the poultry farm and gave the chickens some whisky!

★ CUSTOMER: Waiter, waiter! I've found a caterpillar in my salad!
WAITER: *Don't fuss, sir! It's better than finding half a caterpillar, isn't it?*

★★ Mummy, Mummy! What's for dinner?
Just shut up and get back in the oven . . .

★ ★ When Bill was young his father brought his boss home for dinner one evening. Everyone was on their best behaviour, including Bill, who handed the boss a dish of salted peanuts when his father served drinks before the meal. Then he sat on the floor and stared hard at the visitor.

'What's wrong, Bill?' said his father.

'I'm waiting to see him do his trick,' said Bill.

His father and the boss were puzzled. 'What trick?'

'You said he drinks like a fish, and I want to see it!

★ ★ GRANNY: If you eat your cabbage you'll turn into a beautiful young woman.
KATE: *Why didn't you eat your cabbage when you were a girl, Granny?*

★ CUSTOMER: Waiter, waiter! There's a dead fly in my wine!
WAITER: *Yes, sir — you did ask for something with a little body in it.*

★ CANDY: You should eat more spinach. It's good for the complexion.
KATE: *But who wants a green complexion?*

★ KATE: Would you like to taste this cottage pie?
BEN: *No, thanks. The last time I ate your cottage pie I broke my tooth on a brick.*

★★ CUSTOMER: Waiter, waiter! There's a fly on my burger.
WAITER: *Dear, dear! Those flies will eat anything, won't they?*

★ 'Aha!' said the waiter, when he saw Bill walk into the restaurant. 'We've got just the meal for an idiot like you.'
'What is it,' said Bill, insulted.
'Chump chops.'

★★★ What do you get if you cross a birthday cake with a tin of baked beans?
A cake that blows all the candles out by itself.

★ BEN: Try one of these cakes I've just baked.
KATE (taking a bite): *Urgh! They're horrible!*
BEN: No they're not – the cookery book says they're delicious.

★ CANDY: I believe in a balanced diet.
BEN: *Is that why you always have a hamburger in each hand?*

★ ★ ★ CUSTOMER: Waiter, waiter! This tea tastes like old socks.
WAITER: *That's coffee, sir. The tea tastes like cat's pee.*

★ What do you call rude potatoes?
Fresh vegetables.

★ KATE: I don't know what to make of Bill...
BEN: *How about a nice hotpot?*

★ CUSTOMER: Waiter, waiter! Your thumb is on my roast beef.
WAITER: *Yes, sir, I didn't want to drop it on the floor again.*

★ ★ KATE: Would you like some nouga*t*?
CANDY: *It's nouga*r*, not nouga*t* – the 't' is silent.*
KATE: Not when you eat it, it isn't!

★ ★ CUSTOMER: Waiter, waiter! Is it safe to drink the water in this restaurant?
WAITER: *Certainly, sir. The manager has passed it all himself.*

★ BEN: Since I met you I haven't been able to eat or drink.
CANDY: *Because you love me so much?*
BEN: No, because I don't have any money!

★ CUSTOMER: Waiter, waiter! is this English or Danish bacon?
WAITER: *What do you want to do — eat it or talk to it?*

★ ★ BILL: Why are you crying?
KATE: *I just made a steak and kidney pie and now the cat's eaten it.*
BILL: Don't worry — we can get another cat.

★ ★ What happened to the man who lived on bran and beans?
The bottom dropped out of his world.

★ PATIENT: Doctor, Doctor! I've just eaten a roll of film!
DOCTOR: *Just wait and see what develops.*

83

★ BEN: You remind me of a dishy Italian.
KATE: *Sophia Loren?*
BEN: Er, no — I was thinking of spaghetti.

★★ A waiter served a customer a plate of soup with his thumb sticking in it.

'Careful!' said the customer, 'Your thumb's in my soup.'

'That's because I got rheumatism in this thumb and my doctor told me to keep it warm.'

'Well, stick it in your mouth then.'

'I do when I'm in the kitchen.'

★ BEN: My father's a terrible cook. He's so bad he thought *coq au vin* was a chicken in a lorry.

★ BILL: Our family's getting a cat for Christmas.
CANDY: *Really? Our family always has a turkey.*

★★ KATE: You remind me of a biscuit.
BEN: *A delicious chocolate digestive?*
KATE: No, a gingernut — because you're red-haired and stupid.

★ What was the Czar of Russia's favourite food?
Czardines.

★ BEN: This is the cleanest restaurant I've ever been in.
WAITER: *That's true, sir, but how could you tell?*
BEN: Because everything tastes of soap.

★ A man woke his wife in the middle of the night. 'Wake up!' he whispered. 'I can hear a burglar in the kitchen and he's eating the cake I made yesterday.'
'Who should we call?' asked his wife. 'The police or an ambulance?'

★ CUSTOMER: Waiter, waiter! This trifle tastes funny.
WAITER: *Well, why aren't you laughing?*
CUSTOMER: Waiter, I didn't come here to be insulted!
WAITER: *So where do you usually go?*

★ Why did the idiot eat nothing but biscuits?
Because he was crackers.

★ BEN: We call my mum's cooking 'health food'.
CANDY: *Because it makes you strong and healthy?*
BEN: No – because you have to be healthy to survive it.

★★★ Kate was having lunch at school one day when a teacher came up and asked, 'Is everything all right?'

'No,' said Kate, 'This meat is terribly tough.'

The teacher picked up a fork and took a piece of meat from her plate, tasted it and then said, 'It's not too tough.'

'That's because I'd already chewed it for ten minutes,' said Kate.

★★ BILL: Shall I offer Kate one of my home-made biscuits?
BEN: *Why? What harm has Kate ever done to you?*

★ CANDY: Bill is just like a cabbage.
KATE: *Why do you say that?*
CANDY: He's got a head but no brain.

★ Have you heard about the madman who annoys sweetshop owners by going into the shop pointing at a Mars bar and asking, 'Is this Mars bar for sale?'

'Yes,' they say. 'Do you want it?'

'Maybe,' says the man, 'but I have a few others to see before I make my mind up.'

★★ GRANNY: Did you enjoy the pie?
KATE: *To be honest, it was horrible.*
GRANNY: But I was making pies before you were born!
KATE: *It tastes like it, too.*

★ What do chiropodists eat for breakfast?
Shredded Feet or Corn Flakes.

★ CANDY: Ben's so stupid.
KATE: *What's he done now?*
CANDY: He tried to bake a birthday cake, and all the candles melted in the oven.

★ Bill was talking to Candy about his parents.
'I sometimes moan about my mother's cooking, but you should try my father's.'
'Bad?' asked Candy.
'He even burns Cornflakes.'

★ CUSTOMER: Waiter, waiter! There's a fly in my butter.
WAITER: *No there isn't.*
CUSTOMER: Yes there is!
WAITER: *No there isn't — we only serve margarine in this restaurant.*

★ Is Popeye good at making pizza?
No, he gets Olive Oyl everywhere.

★ ★ CUSTOMER: Waiter, if this meat is beef then I'm a raving idiot!
WAITER: *You're a raving idiot, sir.*

★ ★ KATE: If you were my husband I'd put poison in your coffee.
BEN: *And if I was your husband I'd drink it.*

★ Why don't the Chinese eat custard?
Have you ever tried eating custard with chopsticks, stupid?

★ CANDY: We always say a prayer at our house before we eat.
BEN: *We don't have to at my house – my mum's a good cook,*

★★ CUSTOMER: Waiter, waiter! How do you manage to keep flies out of this restaurant?
WAITER: *That's easy sir – we keep a big bucket of manure in the kitchen.*

★★ KATE: Shall I put the kettle on?
BILL: *Why not? It would look better than that dress.*

★ Why do spiders taste like chewing gum?
Because they're wrigglies.

★★ CANDY: Do you have fried liver and kidneys?
WAITER: *Yes we do, miss.*
CANDY: In that case you'd better see a doctor quickly.

★ 'It looks like rain this morning,' said the waiter as he served Candy with a cup of coffee.

'It tastes like rain, too,' said Candy.

★   KATE: Ben's cooking is getting better.
    CANDY: *You mean you can actually eat what he cooks?*
    KATE: No, but these days the smoke is grey instead of black.

★★ What happened when Cyril Smith fell into the lion enclosure at London Zoo?
    He ate two of them before they could get him out . . .

★★ CANDY: Your face should be painted in oils.
    BEN: *Because I'm so incredibly handsome?*
    CANDY: No – because you've got a face like a sardine.

★★ A man went into a restaurant and asked, 'Have you got asparagus?'
'No, we don't serve sparrows,' said the waiter, 'and if you call me Gus again I'll punch you on the nose!'

★ BILL: It's pouring down with rain outside and the weather forecast says a hurricane's on its way. You'd better stay to dinner.
KATE: *The weather's not that bad.*

★ What happened to the butcher who sat on his bacon slicer?
He got behind with his work.

★ KATE: The food in this place is terrible.
BILL: *Even the dustbin's got ulcers!*

★ CUSTOMER: Waiter, waiter! Do I have to sit here forever until I die of starvation?
WAITER: *No, sir. We'll chuck you out when we close at six.*

★★ GRANDAD: Say grace if you've finished your dinner, Ben.
BEN: *Thanks for dinner, God.*
GRANDAD: That wasn't much good.
BEN: *Neither was dinner.*

RUDE RHYMES

There's nothing like a rude rhyme to cheer you up at difficult moments. Here are some of the cheekiest we could find!

A little birdie flying by.
Dropped a message from the sky.
A passing lady wiped her eye
And said, 'Thank goodness cows can't fly!'

The rain makes everything beautiful.
It makes the flowers blue.
If the rain makes everything beautiful.
Why doesn't it rain on you?

There was an old man from Penzance
Who always wore sheet-steel pants.
He said, 'Some years back
I sat down on a tack,
And I'll never again take a chance!'

Raising frogs for profit
Is a very sorry joke.
How can you make money
When so many of them croak?

I shot a sneeze into the air,
It fell to earth I know not where.
But some days later, so I'm told,
A dozen others caught my cold.

I am a girl guide dressed in blue.
These are the actions I can do.
Salute to the Captain,
Curtsey to the Queen.
Show my knickers to the football team.

There was a young woman called Sue
Who spent most of the day in the loo.
She said, 'All I ate is
A plateful of haggis.
If *you'd* eaten it you'd be here too!'

The rain it raineth on the just
As well as on the unjust fella.
But mostly on the just, because
The unjust's nicked the just's umbrella!

Don't worry if your life's a joke.
And your successes few;
Remember that a mighty oak
Was once a nut like you!

I eat my peas with honey.
I've done so all my life.
It makes the peas taste funny,
But it keeps them on my knife.

There once was a young man from Spain
Who was terribly sick on a train.
Not once, but again
And again and again
And again, and again, and again!

Tommy had a wristwatch.
He swallowed it one day.
So now he's taking laxatives
To pass the time away.

I had written to Aunt Maud,
Who was on a trip abroad,
When I heard she'd died of cramp —
Just too late to save the stamp.

Grandad Moses killed a skunk;
Grandma Moses cooked the skunk;
Baby Moses ate the skunk;
My, how all those Moses stunk!

Little Miss Muffet
Sat on a tuffet,
Eating some Irish stew.
Along came a spider
And sat down beside her,
So she gobbled him up too!

Mary had a little lamb,
A pheasant and some prunes,
A glass of pop,
A piece of pie,
A plate of macaroons.
She also ate two big cream cakes,
A portion of cod's roe –
And when they carried Mary out
her face was white as snow.

There once was an old man from Ealing
Who had an expectorant feeling.
But a sign on the door
Said, DON'T SPIT ON THE FLOOR –
So this rotten chap spat on the ceiling.

There was a young man from Dundee
Who, trouserless, lived in a tree.
And when passersby
Looked up at the sky
He'd wave and call out, 'Look at me!'

Your daddy is a baker,
Your mummy makes the bread.
And you're a little doughnut
With a hole right through your head.

Don't eat school dinners,
Just throw them aside.
A lot of kids didn't,
A lot of kids died.
The meat's made of iron,
The spuds are made of steel.
And if they don't get you,
The pudding will!

Mary had a little lamb,
She also had a bear.
I've often seen her little lamb
But I've never seen her bare!

Sam, Sam, was a dirty old man.
He washed his face in a frying pan,
Combed his hair with a horse's tail
And scratched his bum with his big
toe-nail.

Bill is brave and Bill is gentle,
Bill is strong and Bill is mental.

Ding-dong bell,
Pussy's in the well.
But now we've put Domestos down
So we don't mind the smell!

There once was a fat boy called Sid,
Who ate twenty rats for a quid.
When asked, 'Are you faint?'
He said, 'No, I ain't –
But I don't feel as well as I did!'

Mary had a little lamb,
You've heard this tale before,
But did you know she passed the plate
And had a little more?

Willie, with a thirst for gore,
Nailed his sister to the door.
His mother said, with humour quaint,
'Willie, dear, don't scratch that paint!'

PLAIN YUCK

When I was collecting jokes to include in this book I came across a few that were so disgusting they made me go 'Yuck!'. So I put them all together to make one really yucky chapter. If you don't like yucky things, turn the pages quickly. But if you *do* like yucky jokes you'll love these!

★ What stinks but is useful in a war?
A septic tank.

★★ KATE: Did you hear about the man who jumped into a cesspit?
CANDY: *Yuck! What happened?*
KATE: He committed sewercide.

★★ Doctor, doctor! I've got diarrhoea!
Does it run in your family?

★ ★ ★   A rather posh lady was attending a vicarage tea party. All the guests were in the garden and the vicar's dog was out there too. The dog suddenly sat down and began to scratch the middle of his back with one of his legs.

'I wish I was bendy enough to be able to do that, don't you, vicar?' said the lady, gesturing towards the dog.

The vicar turned to look — and saw the dog licking its bum!

★   CANDY: Have you seen that comedian who does wonderful farmyard inpressions?
BEN: *Can he make all the noises?*
CANDY: No, but he does all the smells.

★ ★ ★   BEN: I never go swimming in the sea.
KATE: *Why not?*
BEN: Because fish pee in it.

★ ★ ★   Knock, knock.
Who's there?
Adjust.
Adjust who?
Adjust made a mess in my trousers.

★ ★   BEN: Tell me you love me or I'll hang myself from that tree in your garden.
CANDY: *Please don't — I hate people hanging around outside.*

★ ★   What's sticky, mucky, covered in blood and floats around in swimming-pools?
A used Band Aid.

★   BEN: Why is your dog called Handyman?
CANDY: *Because he does little jobs around the house.*

★   A woman was having some carpets fitted in her sitting-room. The fitters were doing well and had just finished the job when they noticed a strange lump in the middle of the carpet. 'What's that?' they wondered gloomily, thinking they'd have to take the carpet up and start all over again.

'Oh, I know, it's my bag of crisps,' said one of the workmen. 'I must have left them on the floor when we put down the carpet. Don't worry!' And he took a big hammer and bashed the lump until it went flat.

Just at that moment the lady walked in with a tray of coffee. 'I thought you might like these,' she said. 'I found your crisps in the kitchen if you want them. And by the way, I don't suppose you've seen my daughter's hamster anywhere, have you?'

★ ★ ★ KATE: Ben's always in a terrible mood when he's eaten baked beans for lunch.
BILL: *Is he really?*
KATE: He raises a stink all afternoon.

★ ★ Mummy, Mummy! I don't like Daddy.
Then leave him on the side of the plate and finish your chips.'

★ ★ What's green and red and can be sucked up through a straw?
A liquidized frog.

★ ★ ★ 'Doctor, doctor!' cried the patient as he ran into the surgery. 'I've got a terrible case of diahorrea.'
'When did you notice it?' asked the doctor.
'Just now, when I took off my bicycle clips.'

★ CANDY: Mrs Nitwit's just had her fingers chopped off.
BILL: *Yuck! Why?*
CANDY: So that she can write shorthand.

★★ KATE: My boyfriend's such a coward that I asked him to prove he's got guts.
CANDY: *How did he do that?*
KATE: He lay down in front of a lawnmower.

★★ What's the nearest thing to Silver?
The Lone Ranger's bum.

★ BILL: Is there a difference between Grandad's home-made stew and dog food?
CANDY: *Yes — the stew is served on a plate and the dog food comes in a dish.*

★★ Ben was baby-sitting for his little sister one day. 'Give her anything she wants to eat,' his mum said as she went out. 'That way she won't make a fuss.' So at teatime Ben asked little Annie what she'd like.

'A caterpillar,' she said.

'A caterpillar?'

'A caterpillar – and if you don't let me have one I'll scream and scream.' Ben remembered what his mum had said, so he went out to the garden, found a caterpillar and put it on a plate.

'You eat half first,' said his little sister when he saw it.

'Oh, yuck!' moaned Ben. But he picked up his knife and fork, sliced the caterpillar in two and ate half of it. 'There!' he spluttered,' the other half's for you.'

'But you ate the bit with the head!' said his sister. 'I wanted that half – but never mind, I'll have fish fingers instead.'

★ Mummy, Mummy! I don't want to go to America!
Just shut up and keep swimming!

★★★ What's brown and smelly and sounds like a bell?
Dung.

★ ★ What should you give a constipated budgie? *Chirrup of figs.*

★ ★ ★ KATE: Do you know the difference between a toilet and a handbasin?
BILL: *No, what's the difference?*
KATE: If you don't know, you're not going to the loo at my house!

★ Did you hear what happened to the blind skunk? He fell in love with a sewer pipe.

★ ★ A crazy man walked into the dentist's. 'Would you take all my teeth out?' he asked.
'But there's nothing wrong with them,' said the dentist.
'I don't care. Just take them out,' said the crazy man. 'And I don't want any anaesthetic to dull the pain. Pull them out slowly.'
So the dentist did as he was told and slowly pulled out all the man's teeth. As the last one came out in the pliers, the crazy guy jumped up from the chair.
'Fooled you!' he laughed. 'I didn't really want all my teeth pulled out without an injection – I just came in for a new toothbrush!'

★★★ 'Why are you late for church parade?' asked the Brownie leader.

'I'm sorry,' said the Brownie, 'but as I was passing Farmer Jones' field of cows my beret flew off.'

'But why did it take so long to get it back? said Brown Owl crossly.

'I had to try six times before I found it.'

★★ BILL: You know, Walls really do have ears.
BEN: *How do you know?*
BILL: I just found one in my pork pie.

★ What did the boy maggot say to the girl maggot?
'What are you doing in a rotten joint like this?'

★   BEN: I've just bought a piglet. I think I'll keep it under my bed.
    BILL: *But what about the smell?*
    BEN: It'll just have to get used to it.

★   PATIENT: Doctor, doctor! I've got a terrible pain where I sit down.
    DOCTOR: *All right, let's get to the bottom of this.*

★   DOCTOR: I'm sorry to tell you that your little Billy has been run over by a steam roller.
    MRS MONSTER: *Oh dear! Just slide him under the door, will you?*

★ ★ 'What did you buy Kate for her birthday?' asked Bill.

'A bottle of toilet water,' answered Ben. 'It cost me £12.'

'£12! That's outrageous! If you'd come to my house you could have had a whole bucket from our toilet for free!'

★   What happens when you cross a boomerang and a skunk?
    A terrible pong that won't go away.

★ ★ BILL: How much does dinner cost here?
WAITER: *It's £10 a head.*
BILL: In that case I'll just have an eyeball and an ear.

★ Mummy, Mummy! I don't like Billy.
Then put some more tomato ketchup on him.

★ ★ NEWSFLASH... A lorryload of prunes and a van full of bran have been stolen from a car park in Manchester. Police say the thieves are still on the run.

★ ★ ★ BILL: I've got a dirty magazine
BEN: *With rude pictures?*
BILL: No, it fell in some dog mess.

★ ★ ★ What's brown and comes steaming out of Cowes?
The Isle of Wight ferry.

★ ★ KATE: What's the difference between a doughnut and a dead frog?
CANDY: *I don't know.*
KATE: Okay, I'll eat the doughnut and you can have the frog.

★★ Knock, knock
Who's there?
Sonya.
Sonya who?
Sonya shoe! I can smell it from here!

★ CANDY: I love Bros.
BILL: *Fried or grilled?*

INSULTING BEHAVIOUR

There's nothing like a really good insult — unless you're on the receiving end of it! Have a giggle at some of these rude replies and who knows, maybe you'll find they come in useful one day.

★ ★   KATE: You have a heart of gold.
BILL: *You mean I'm kind and considerate?*
KATE: No, you're hard and yellow.

★ ★   BEN: Don't look out of the window, please.
CANDY: *Why not?*
BEN: I don't want anyone to think it's Hallowe'en.

★ Why don't you stop acting like an idiot?
Who's acting?

★★ KATE: I've got a new baby brother! The stork brought him yesterday.
BILL: *He's so ugly I bet a vulture brought him.*

★ CANDY: Say something soft and sweet to me.
BEN: *Marshmallows, treacle, sponge cake ...*

★★ KATE: Do you like me?
BILL: *Well, as girls go you're okay. And the further you go, the better.*

★ CANDY: What's your worst fault?
BEN: *I suppose it's vanity. I like to sit in front of the mirror and admire my handsome face.*
CANDY: That's not vanity — it's a vivid imagination.

★★ I'm speechless.
Great! Just stay that way.

★ BEN: Gosh, I'm so thirsty my tongue's hanging out!
BILL: *Is that your tongue? I thought it was a horrible spotty tie.*

★ KATE: I have the skin of a baby.
BILL: *Well, you'd better give it back — it's getting wrinkled.*

★★ BEN: Your ears are like petals.
CANDY: *Rose petals?*
BEN: I was thinking of bicycle petals.

★★ BILL: This cream the doctor's given me makes my spots smart.
BEN: *Why don't you rub some on your head?*

★ CANDY: I'm nobody's fool.
BILL: *Perhaps we could find someone to adopt you?*

★ ★   BEN: Your big sister has such a sympathetic face.
CANDY: *What do you mean by that?*
BEN: Well, whenever I look at her I feel sympathetic for her.

★ ★   MR TWIT: Can you give me something to help my baldness?
DOCTOR: *How about rubbing in a pound of cow manure and fifty cloves of garlic?*
MR TWIT: Will that stop my hair falling out?
DOCTOR: *No, but no one will get close enough to spot that you're going bald.*

★ ★   BEN: You know, Kate didn't like me when we first met but I gradually grew on her.
CANDY: *Like a wart.*

★   CANDY: My Dad's teeth are like stars.
BEN: *Do they sparkle?*
CANDY: No, but they come out at night.

★ ★   KATE: Boys fall in love with me at first sight.
CANDY: *Yes — it's only at the second look they decide they can't stand you.*

★ ★ KATE: I want a dress to match my eyes.
BEN: *Are bloodshot dresses fashionable?*

★ ★ MR TWIT: Where are you running off to?
MR WITNIT: *The doctor's — I don't like the look of my wife.*
MR TWIT: Can I come with you? I don't like mine either.

★ BILL: Last night I dreamed I went dancing with the world's most beautiful girl.
CANDY: *And what was I wearing?*

★ BEN: I wouldn't say my girlfriend has a big mouth . . .
BILL: *But when she yawns her ears disappear.*

★ CANDY: I wish you were on television.
BEN: *Would you love me if I was a TV star?*
CANDY: No, but at least I could switch you off.

★ ★ BEN: Waiter, do you have frogs' legs?
WAITER: *Yes, sir.*
BEN: Then hop off and get me a pizza.

★   BILL: How can you be sure your mother hates you?
    BEN: *Why else would she pack a road map with my sandwiches every day?*

★   CANDY: I'll have you know I've got a mind of my own.
    BILL: *Only because no one else wants to borrow it.*

★   BEN: You're such a nice bird.
    KATE: *I must be if I'm going out with a worm like you.*

★ ★   BILL: One of the best things about me is that I throw myself into everything I undertake.
    BEN: *Then why don't you go and dig a big hole?*

★   CANDY: Every time Ben and I go out for a meal he eats his head off.
    KATE: *Don't worry! He looks better that way.*

★★ KATE: Has anyone ever told you you have a face like a saint?
BEN: *Have I really?*
KATE: Yes – a St Bernard.

★★ Bill and Ben were at a disco. 'Have you noticed that girl over there?' asked Bill. 'She's wearing eyeshadow and mascara but no lipstick.'

'That's because she can't keep her mouth still for long enough to put it on.'

★ KATE: Could you be happy with a girl like me?
BEN: *Maybe – if you weren't around too often.*

★ CANDY: You remind me of the wild blue oceans.
BILL: *Because I'm wild, untamable and romantic?*
CANDY: No – because you make me feel sick.

★ CANDY: My boyfriend's different from all the other men in the world.
KATE: *Quite right — he's the only one who'll go out with you.*

★★ BEN: Your face should be on the cover of a magazine.
KATE: *Vogue, Hair and Beauty. . . ?*
BEN: I was thinking more of *Pigeon Fancier's Monthly*.

★ BILL: The computer dating agency selected me as the ideal boyfriend.
KATE: *But who wants to go out with a computer?*

★ BILL: My girlfriend's a woman of many parts.
KATE: *Pity no one put them together properly.*

★ What's your grandpa getting for Christmas?
Balder.

★ KATE: Call me a taxi.
CANDY: *Okay, you're a taxi!*

★ ★ CANDY: If frozen water is called iced water, what's frozen ink?
BEN: *Iced ink.*
CANDY: Yes, you do!

★ BEN: You remind me of the Venus de Milo.
KATE: *Do I really?*
BEN: Yes — beautiful but not all there.

★ BEN: Are you trying to make a fool of me?
BILL: *No, I believe in leaving nature alone.*

★ BILL: I'm one of those people who believe that looks aren't everything.
KATE: *In your case, they're not anything!*

★ CANDY: Bill has a real chip on his shoulder.
BEN: *Yes, it comes from the block of wood on his neck.*

★ Candy and Kate were out shopping one day and discussing their boyfriends.
'He keeps saying he'd die for me,' said Candy. 'The problem is, he never does.'

★ BILL: Ouch! I've got a splinter.
KATE: *I keep telling you not to scratch your head.*

★★ CANDY: What's that disgusting lump on your neck?
BILL: *What do you mean?*
CANDY: Whoops! It's your head!

★ I've got a great idea!
Hmm, beginner's luck.

★★ BEN: I love nature.
BILL: *That's very kind, considering what nature has done to you!*

★★ KATE: Mrs Nitwit's so stupid, she can't see beyond the end of her nose.
BEN: *Mmmm — but with her nose that's quite a long way.*

★ CANDY: Would you say that Ben was arrogant?
KATE: *Well, I sometimes feel sorry for his poor little brain stuck all alone in that big head . . .*

★ BILL: Candy calls me 'Angel'.
BEN: *Only because you're always harping on about things.*

★★ KATE: Oooh, I feel like a cup of tea!
CANDY: *And you look like one too — all wet and sloppy.*

★ BILL: My mother thinks I'm a great wit.
BEN: *Well, I'd say she's half right.*

★★ KATE: My boyfriend says that I'm beautiful.
BEN: *Well, they say love is blind.*

★ CANDY: How could I ever leave you?
BILL: *Well, you could go by plane, bus, bicycle, coach, hovercraft, roller skates . . .*

★ Knock, knock.
Who's there?
Phil.
Phil who?
Philthy dirty, that's who!

★★ KATE: I want to be a movie star. I want to see my name up in lights in the cinema.
BILL: *How about changing your name to Toilets?*

★ I've changed my mind.
I know — I've noticed the improvement.

★ CANDY: My old boyfriend was nicknamed Caterpillar.
BILL: *Because he's green and squashy?*
CANDY: No, because he's such a crawler.

★ BEN: Your tights are all wrinkly.
KATE: *I'm not wearing tights!*

★ What is it rude to call a woman with one leg?
Eileen.

★ BILL: Candy says that whenever she's down in the dumps she gets herself a new pair of shoes.
KATE: *I've always wondered where she got them!*

★★ CANDY: Some people say I'm as pretty as a flower.
BILL: *A cauliflower, maybe.*

★ BEN: Will you love me when I'm old and wrinkly?
KATE: *Yes, I do!*

★ Bill and Kate went to a restaurant one night. There was a terrible band playing awful old-fashioned tunes, so Bill called the waiter over and said, 'Does your band play requests?'

'Yes, sir,' said the waiter.

'In that case ask them to play Trivial Pursuit until we've finished our meal.'

★ CANDY: I don't know what's wrong with me today. I can't stop talking to myself.
BEN: *That must be why you're looking so bored!*

★ KATE: How does your head feel today?
BILL: *As good as new.*
KATE: That doesn't surprise me – after all, it's never been used.

★ BILL: You know, Kate's a model girlfriend.
BEN: *Pity she's not a working model.*

★ CANDY: Your face reminds me of a Bournemouth guest house in January.
BILL: *Why?*
CANDY: It's vacant.

★★ OLD LADY: Can you see me across the road, young man?
BILL: *Of course I can, I've got perfect eyesight.*

★★ BEN: It's not that Kate's not pretty, but I sometimes think that if I pulled her pigtail she'd go, 'Oink!'

★ KATE: I went to the zoo yesterday.
BEN: *That's amazing! So did I.*
KATE: Strange — I looked in all the cages and I didn't see you!

★ CANDY: You remind me of a fence.
BEN: *Oh, really?*
CANDY: Yes you run around but you never get anywhere.

Other great reads from **Red Fox**

Further Red Fox titles that you might enjoy reading are listed on the following pages. They are available in bookshops or they can be ordered directly from us.

If you would like to order books, please send this form and the money due to:

ARROW BOOKS, BOOKSERVICE BY POST, PO BOX 29, DOUGLAS, ISLE OF MAN, BRITISH ISLES. Please enclose a cheque or postal order made out to Arrow Books Ltd for the amount due, plus 30p per book for postage and packing to a maximum of £3.00, both for orders within the UK. For customers outside the UK, please allow 35p per book.

NAME _____

ADDRESS _____

_____

Please print clearly.

Whilst every effort is made to keep prices low, it is sometimes necessary to increase cover prices at short notice. If you are ordering books by post, to save delay it is advisable to phone to confirm the correct price. The number to ring is THE SALES DEPARTMENT 071 (if outside London) 973 9700.

Other great reads from Red Fox

Two books from Enid Blyton

THE BIRTHDAY KITTEN *and* THE BOY WHO WANTED A DOG—2 books in 1!

The Birthday Kitten

Terry and Tessie, the twins, want a pet of their own very badly. While they are playing with Terry's new boat, they notice a small, wriggling bundle in the pond. It is a tiny, half-drowned kitten. But what will their mother say when they take it home?

The Boy who Wanted a Dog

Donald's parents won't let him have a dog, but he's allowed to help out at the local vet's kennels—until his father bans him for neglecting his homework.

Sadly, Donald goes down to the kennels for one last time . . . and what a good thing it is that he does!

ISBN 0 09 977930 7 £1.99

THE GOBLIN AEROPLANE AND OTHER STORIES

'The strange aeroplane flew swiftly towards them, flapping its odd red and yellow wings . . .'

It is such a nice day that Jill and Robert are doing their spelling lessons out of doors. Before they know what is happening they are whisked away in a goblin aeroplane into a strange adventure.

This book brings together a delightful and varied collection of magical stories which will provide hours of entertainment.

ISBN 0 09 973590 3 £1.99

Other great reads from **Red Fox**

THE SNIFF STORIES   Ian Whybrow

Things just keep happening to Ben Moore. It's dead hard avoiding disaster when you've got to keep your street cred with your mates *and* cope with a family of oddballs at the same time. There's his appalling 2½ year old sister, his scatty parents who are into healthy eating and animal rights and, worse than all of these, there's Sniff! If only Ben could just get on with his scientific experiments and his attempt at a world beating *Swampbeast* score . . . but there's no chance of that while chaos is just around the corner.

ISBN 0 09 9750406   £2.50

J.B. SUPERSLEUTH   Joan Davenport

James Bond is a small thirteen-year-old with spots and spectacles. But with a name like that, how can he help being a supersleuth?

It all started when James and 'Polly' (Paul) Perkins spotted a teacher's stolen car. After that, more and more mysteries needed solving. With the case of the Arabian prince, the Murdered Model, the Bonfire Night Murder and the Lost Umbrella, JB's reputation at Moorside Comprehensive soars.

But some of the cases aren't quite what they seem . . .

ISBN 0 09 9717808   £1.99

Other great reads from **Red Fox**

Discover the exciting and hilarious books of Hazel Townson!

THE MOVING STATUE

One windy day in the middle of his paper round, Jason Riddle is blown against the town's war memorial statue.

But the statue moves its foot! Can this be true?

ISBN 0 09 973370 6   £1.99

ONE GREEN BOTTLE

Tim Evans has invented a fantasic new board game called REDUNDO. But after he leaves it at his local toy shop it disappears! Could Mr Snyder, the wily toy shop owner have stolen the game to develop it for himself? Tim and his friend Doggo decide to take drastic action and with the help of a mysterious green bottle, plan a Reign of Terror.

ISBN 0 09 956810 1   £1.50

THE SPECKLED PANIC

When Kip buys Venger's Speckled Truthpaste instead of toothpaste, funny things start happening. But they get out of control when the headmaster eats some by mistake. What terrible truths will he tell the parents on speech day?

ISBN 0 09 935490 X   £1.75

THE CHOKING PERIL

In this sequel to *The Speckled Panic*, Herbie, Kip and Arthur Venger the inventor attempt to reform Grumpton's litterbugs.

ISBN 0 09 950530 4   £1.25

Other great reads from **Red Fox**

The latest and funniest joke books are from Red Fox!

THE OZONE FRIENDLY JOKE BOOK
Kim Harris, Chris Langham, Robert Lee, Richard Turner

What's green and highly dangerous?
How do you start a row between conservationists?
What's green and can't be rubbed out?

Green jokes for green people (non-greens will be pea-green when they see how hard you're laughing), bags and bags of them (biodegradable of course).

All the jokes in this book are printed on environmentally friendly paper and every copy you buy will help GREENPEACE save our planet.

* David Bellamy with a machine gun.
* Pour oil on troubled waters.
* The Indelible hulk.

ISBN 0 09 973190 8   £1.99

THE HAUNTED HOUSE JOKE BOOK
John Hegarty

There are skeletons in the scullery . . .
Beasties in the bath . . .
There are spooks in the sitting room
And jokes to make you laugh . . .

Search your home and see if we are right. Then come back, sit down and shudder to the hauntingly funny and eerily rib-rattling jokes in this book.

ISBN 0 09 9621509   £1.99